100 LEAD LICKS FOR GUITAR

Published by
Wise Publications
14-15 Berners Street,
London W1T 3LJ, UK.

Exclusive Distributors:
Music Sales Limited
Distribution Centre, Newmarket Road,
Bury St Edmunds, Suffolk IP33 3YB, UK.
Music Sales Corporation
257 Park Avenue South,
New York, NY 10010, USA.
Music Sales Pty Limited
20 Resolution Drive, Caringbah,
NSW 2229, Australia.

Order No. AM999471
ISBN 978-1-84938-387-5

All guitar licks & solos written, arranged,
played and recorded by Alan Warner.

Photos courtesy of LFI.
Cover design by Ruth Keating.

Printed in the EU.

Your Guarantee of Quality
As publishers, we strive to produce every book to the
highest commercial standards.
This book has been carefully designed to minimise awkward
page turns and to make playing from it a real pleasure.
Particular care has been given to specifying acid-free,
neutral-sized paper made from pulps which have not been
elemental chlorine bleached.
This pulp is from farmed sustainable forests and was
produced with special regard for the environment.
Throughout, the printing and binding have been planned to
ensure a sturdy, attractive publication which should give
years of enjoyment.
If your copy fails to meet our high standards,
please inform us and we will gladly replace it.

www.musicsales.com

ALAN WARNER was born in Paddington, London.
He started playing guitar at the age of 11. After leaving
school at 14, Alan played with several
semi-pro bands, before turning professional at 16.
He turned down an offer to join The Black Eagles, with
Phil Lynott, who later went on to form
Thin Lizzy. His first big break came when he went on
tour backing Edwin Starr. He had several
international hit records with the hugely successful
multi-racial band The Foundations, producing hits such
as 'Baby Now That I've Found You',
'Build Me Up Buttercup' and 'Bad Bad Old Days'.
He was also in the highly acclaimed 70s rock band
Pluto, whose albums are still selling worldwide today.
Alan is still very busy playing with different bands as well
as teaching guitar and writing guitar books and DVDs.

WISE PUBLICATIONS
PART OF THE MUSIC SALES GROUP
LONDON / NEW YORK / PARIS / SYDNEY / COPENHAGEN / BERLIN / MADRID / TOKYO

CD TRACKLISTING

ROCK LICKS

Track 1
00:00 Tuning Notes
01:36 1. Rock Lick In A

Track 2
2. Rock Lick In A

Track 3
3. Rock Lick In A

Track 4
4. Rock Boogie Lick In A

Track 5
5. Rock Lick In D Minor

Track 6
6. Rock Lick In D Minor

Track 7
7. Boogie Lick In A

Track 8
8. Boogie Lick In D

Track 9
9. Rock Shuffle Lick In E

Track 10
00:00 10. Rockabilly Riff In E
00:42 Rock Guitar Solo In Key Of A 'Move Along'

ROCK INTROS/OUTROS AND TURNAROUNDS

Track 11
11. Rhythm & Blues Intro In A

Track 12
12. Rhythm & Blues Intro/Turnaround

Track 13
13. Turnaround Lick In A

Track 14
14. Flash Rock Intro/Turnaround

Track 15
15. Outro Lick In A

BLUES LICKS

Track 16
16. G Blues Lick

Track 17
17. G Blues Lick

Track 18
18. G Blues Lick

Track 19
19. C Blues Lick

Track 20
20. D Minor Blues Lick

Track 21
21. C Blues Lick

Track 22
22. Blues Lick In A

Track 23
23. Slow Blues In B Minor

Track 24
24. Blues Lick In B Minor

Track 25
25. E Blues Lick

Track 26
26. Fast Blues Shuffle In A

BLUES INTROS/OUTROS AND TURNAROUNDS

Track 27
27. Intro In G

Track 28
28. Turnaround In A

Track 29
29. Turnaround In A

Track 30
30. Intro/Turnaround In A

Track 31
31. Outro In C

Track 32
32. Outro In C

Track 33
33. Intro In G

Track 34
00:00 34. Outro In G
00:35 Rock Guitar Solo In Key Of G 'Going Out Blues'

COUNTRY LICKS

Track 35
35. G Country Lick

Track 36
36. G Country Lick

Track 37
37. G Country Lick

Track 38
38. G Country Lick

Track 39
39. Country Lick In C

Track 40
40. Country Lick In C

Track 41
41. Country Lick In C

Track 42
42. Banjo Type Lick In D

Track 43
43. Banjo Type Lick In G

Track 44
44. Country Rock Lick In A

Track 45
45. Country Rock Lick In A

Track 46
46. Pedal Steel Lick In G

Track 47
47. Pedal Steel Lick In E

Track 48
00:00 48. Pedal Steel Lick In F
00:33 Country Solo In Key Of G 'Southern Bound'

COUNTRY INTROS/OUTROS AND TURNAROUNDS

Track 49
49. Intro In G

Track 50
50. Outro In G

Track 51
51. Outro In A

Track 52
52. Outro Lick In C

Track 53
53. Country Rag Turnaround In C

Track 54
54. Outro In G

Track 55
55. Click Note

Track 56
56. Trill

Track 57
57. Click-Note/Trill Exercise

Track 58
58. Funky Riff In B♭

Track 59
59. B♭ Funky Riff

Track 60
60. E Funk Riff

Track 61
61. Funky Chord Riff In A

Track 62
62. Funk Riff In E

Track 63
00:00 63. Funk Riff In E
00:18 Funk Solo In Key Of B♭ 'Feelin' Funky'

SCALE MODES

Track 64
64. G Ionian

Track 65
65. A Dorian

Track 66
66. B Phrygian

Track 67
67. C Lydian

Track 68
68. D Mixolydian

Track 69
69. E Aeolian

Track 70
70. F# Locrian

Track 71
71. G Ionian

ARPEGGIOS

Track 72
72. A Major

Track 73
73. A Minor

Track 74
74. A Diminished 7Th

Track 75
75. A Major Sweep Arpeggio

Track 76
76. A7

Track 77
77. Heavy Metal Lick In A

Track 78
78. Descending Lick In E

Track 79
79. Ascending Lick In E7

Track 80.
80. Power Chord Riff In A

Track 81
81. Power Chord Riff In A

Track 82
82. Power Chord Riff In D

SPEED EXERCISES

Track 83
83. Speed Exercise In G

Track 84
84. Speed Exercise In G

Track 85
85. Speed Exercise In A

Track 86
86. Speed Exercise In A Minor

Track 87
87. Speed Lick In A Minor

Track 88
88. Speed Lick In E Minor

Track 89
89. Speed Lick In D Minor

Track 90
90. Speed Lick In D Minor

TWO-HAND FRETTING

Track 91
91. Right-Hand Hammer-On

Track 92
92. Right-Hand Hammer-On

Track 93
93. Right-Hand 'Capo'

Track 94
94. Right-Hand 'Capo' Slam

Track 95
95. Right-Hand Hammer-On Lick In A Minor

Track 96
96. Right-Hand Hammer-On Lick In E

Track 97
97. Right-Hand Hammer-On Lick In G

Track 98
98. Right-Hand Hammer-On Lick In A

Track 99
00:00 99. Right-Hand Capo Slam In A
00:18 100. Right-Hand Capo Lick In D
00:51 Heavy Metal Solo In Key Of A 'Time For Change'

Please note: This audio has been digitally transferred from the original cassette supplied with the first edition of this book. In order to match the numbering of each lick it has been necessary to group some sections on the same track.

Contents

Rock

Rock Licks: Numbers 1–10.. 6

Move Along (Rock Solo), Rock Intros, Outros and
Turnarounds: Numbers 11–15.. 11

Blues

Blues Licks: Numbers 16–26... 17

Blues, Outros and Turnarounds: Numbers 27–34.................. 21

Going Out Blues (Blues Solo)... 23

Country

G Major and C Major Country Scale..................................... 27

Country Licks: Numbers 35–48.. 28

Southern Bound (Country Solo)... 35

Country Intros, Outros and Turnarounds: Numbers 49–54.... 40

Funk

Funk Licks: Numbers 55–63.. 41

Feelin' Funky (Funk Solo)... 44

Heavy Metal

Scale Modes: Numbers 64–71 48

Arpeggios: Numbers 72–76... 49

Heavy Metal Licks: Numbers 77–90.................................... 50

Two Hand Fretting Licks: Numbers 91–100 56

Time For Change (Heavy Metal Solo)................................... 61

Symbols (General)

1 Hammer-on

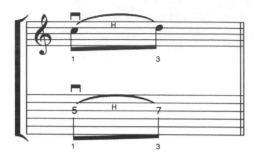

Sound a note as normal then hammer
your LH finger down hard onto the next
note to perform a hammer-on.

2 Pull-off

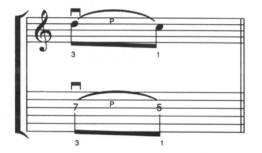

The pull-off is achieved by pulling
your LH finger down off the string
to create the next note.

⌒ P ⌒ means pull-off.

3 Upward String Bend

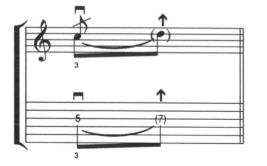

To perform an upward string bend first strike
the note, then push the string up to raise
its pitch. It will then sound at the pitch of the
bracketed note. An upward string bend will
normally be used on the 1st, 2nd or 3rd strings.
The upward arrow indicates an upward string bend.

4 Downward String Bend

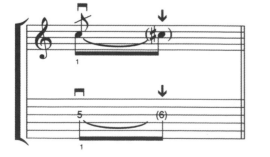

For a downward string bend, pull the string
down to raise its pitch. A downward string bend
will normally be used on the 3rd, 4th, 5th or 6th strings.
The downward arrow indicates a downward string bend.

Striking Or Plucking The Strings

⊓ = Pick downwards with the plectrum.
V = Pick upwards with the plectrum.
p = Pluck downwards with your thumb.
i = Pluck upwards with your index finger.
m = Pluck upwards with your middle finger.
a = Pluck upwards with your ring finger.

5 Slide Going Up

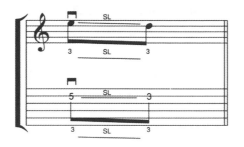

Strike the first note and slide up to the next.

6 Slide Coming Down

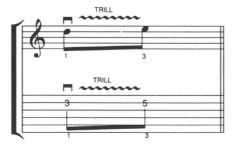

Strike the first note and slide down to the next.

7 Trill

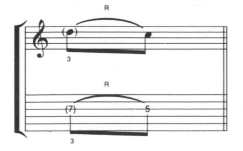

A trill effect is produced by performing hammer-ons and pull-offs in rapid succession.

8 Release String Bend

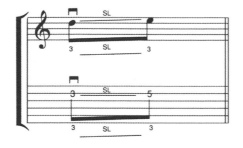

Return from an upward or downward string bend note by releasing the string to its normal position.

1. Rock Lick In A

Here is a rock lick in A using hammer-ons, pull-offs and a slide. It is quite easy to play. Notice how the slide at the end takes you out of the 'box' pattern.

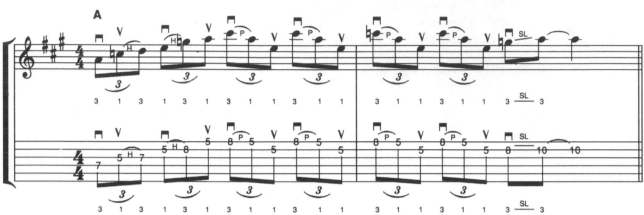

2. Rock Lick In A

This is a classic rock lick which has been used by most famous rock guitarists at one time or another. You will need plenty of practice to make it sound fluent.

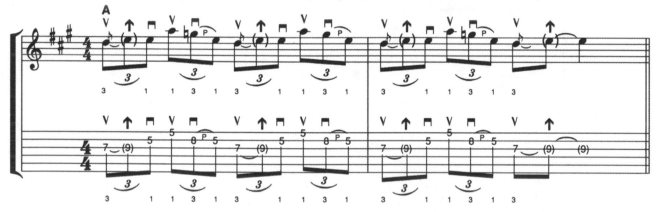

3. Rock Lick In A

This lick is fairly straight forward but be careful when releasing the first string bend (2nd measure). Try to stop the note from sounding when you release it.

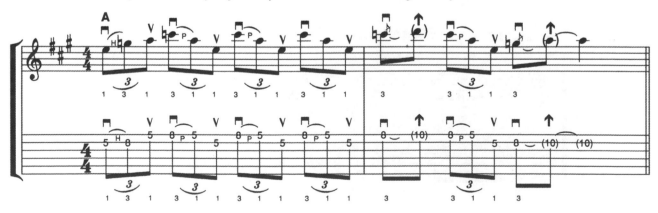

4. Rock Boogie Lick In A

This is a great little guitar lick which will keep your fingers constantly on the move.

5. Rock Lick In D minor

Here is a guitar lick in the style of Mark Knopfler from Dire Straits. Although it is quite long (8 measures altogether), it shouldn't prove too difficult to master.

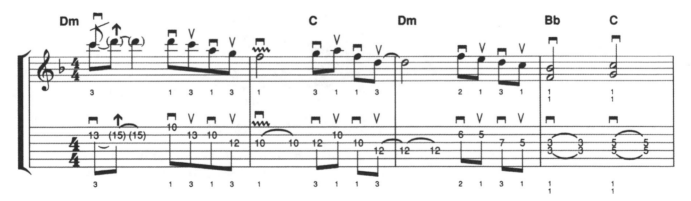

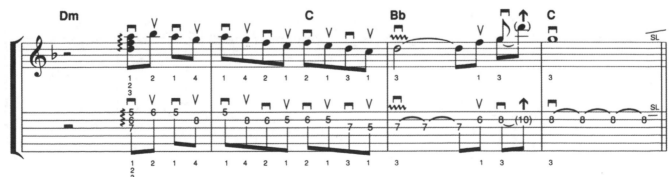

6. Rock Lick In D minor

This lick, which is also in the style of Mark Knopfler, is played against a chord progression of Dm – C – Bb – A. You may find it a little tricky in the 4th measure where you have to change positions to play the two fret string bend up then down.

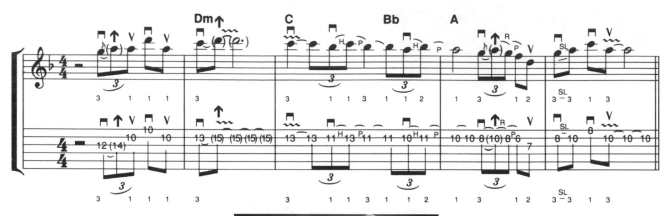

Mark Knopfler

7. Boogie Lick In A

I think you will enjoy this boogie lick as it involves a lot of moving around the fretboard, starting with a slide onto the 9th fret of the 1st (E) string and finishing on the 3rd fret of the 6th (E) string. It covers an area of 8 frets.

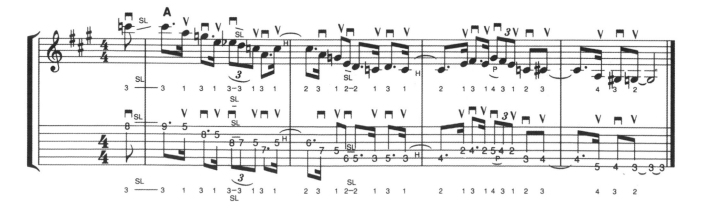

8. Boogie Lick In D

The first half of this lick is quite straight forward but you may find the second part a little more difficult. It is probably a good idea to work on the second half separately for a while.
Make sure you start the second half with the 2 fret string bend at the end of this 2nd measure.

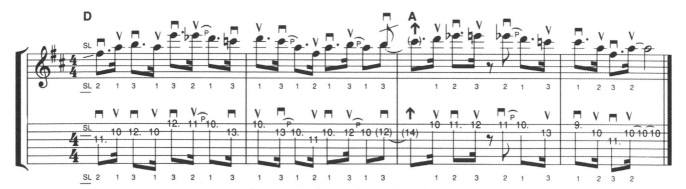

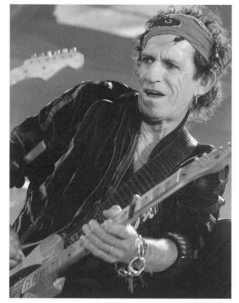

Keith Richards

9. Rock Shuffle Lick In E

This lick which combines both fretted and open string notes,
ends with a 'triplet feel' rock shuffle rhythm.

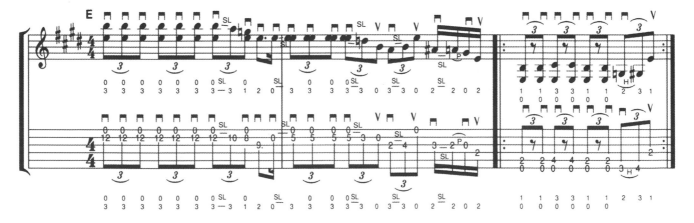

Eddie Cochran

10. Rockabilly Riff In E

This is a great way to start a song or solo and is very useful between the verses of a song.

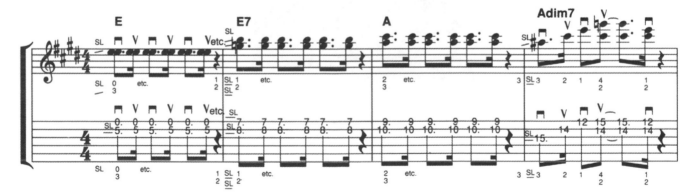

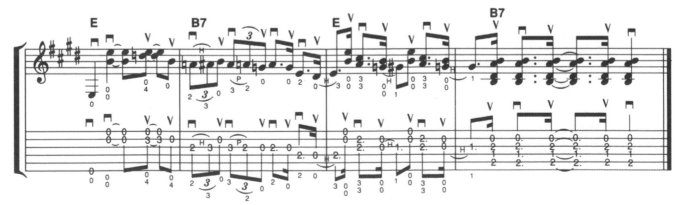

Move Along
written by Alan Warner

Now try playing **Move Along** which is a longer piece comprising some of the licks you have been practising. Here is its layout: **Move Along** starts with a Rhythm 'n Blues Intro Lick in A. (Lick No. 11 from the Intros, Outros and Turnarounds, see page 16) Section 1 starts on the third measure with an A Power Chord. The Middle 8 section uses Lick No. 5 (Rock Lick in D minor). This is followed by a slide going up then coming down. Section 2 begins with a pre-bend whereby the first note is already bent up then released onto the next note.

Middle 8 (same as for Section 1)

Slide (same as Section 1)

Section 3 starts in a similar way to Section 2.

Section 4 ends with Outro Lick No 15 see page 16 and finishes the solo.

Have Fun!

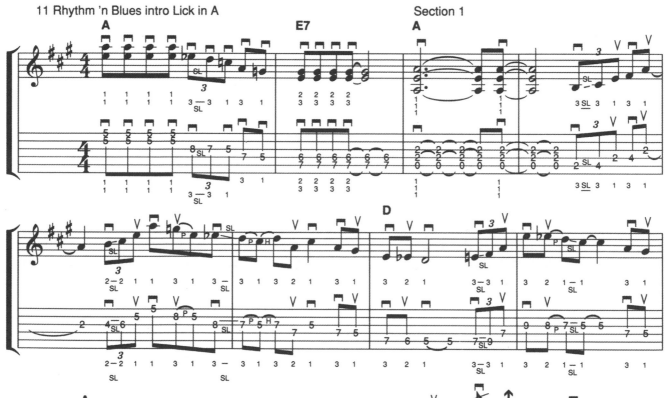

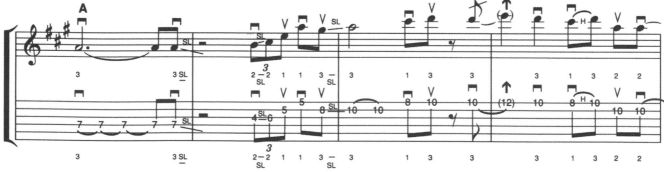

5 Rock Lick In D Minor

Section 2

5 Rock Lick in D minor

13

Section 4

15 Outro Lick In A _ _ _ _ _ _ _ _ _ _ _ _ _

Rock Intros/Outros And Turnarounds

11. Rhythm & Blues Intro In A

12. Rhythm And Blues Intro/Turnaround

13. Turnaround Lick In A

14. Flash Rock Intro/Turnaround

15. Outro Lick In A

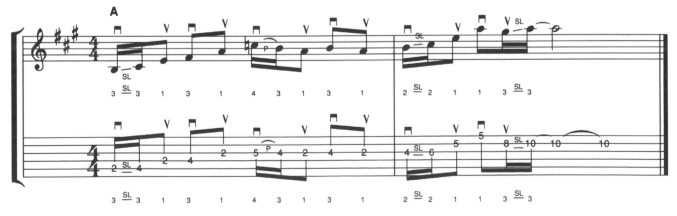

B.B. King

16. G Blues Lick

This **slow** blues lick is quite easy. It is typical of the B. B. King and Eric Clapton style of playing.

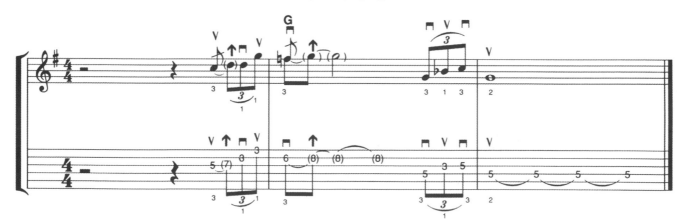

17. G Blues Lick

Here is a Chicago blues lick. When you play the two fret string bends in the second measure make sure that you can't hear them being released.

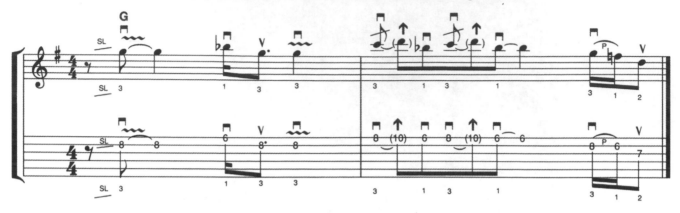

18. G Blues Lick

This is another Chicago blues lick. Notice the release bend followed by a pull-off in the second measure.

19. C Blues Lick

This lick in the style of Robert Cray and Freddie King features a three fret bend followed by a tricky bit containing hammer-ons and pull-offs. It may take some time to master.

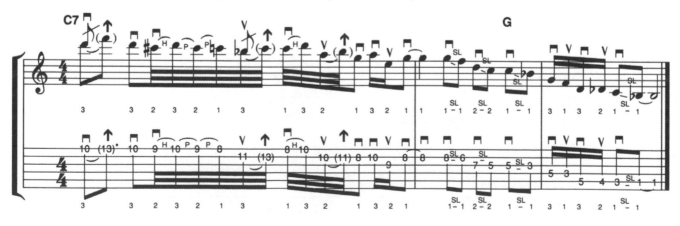

20. D minor Blues Lick

Aim for a hard, almost mechanical sound here.

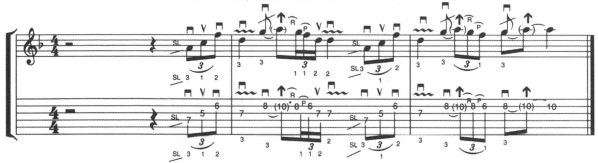

21. C Blues Lick

The notes for this lick are based on the C Major Pentatonic Scale.

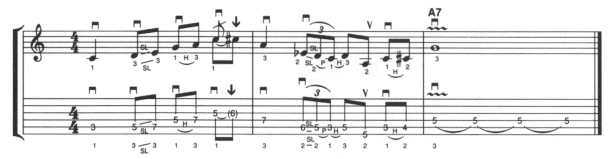

22. Blues Lick In A

23. Slow Blues in B minor

This lick has a rather jazzy sound and is played to a slow tempo, although the notes in the first measure are played quite fast.

24. Blues Lick in B minor

Here's another jazzy sounding blues lick.

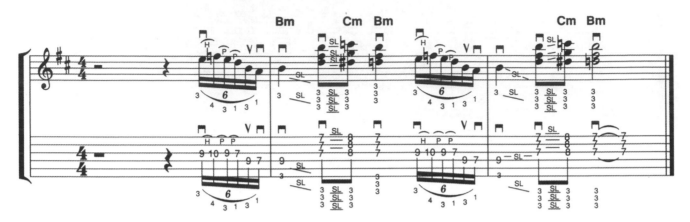

25. E Blues Lick

This slow earthy type of blues lick is typical of the Muddy Waters and Howling Wolf style of guitar playing. It is played with a slow and deliberate beat.

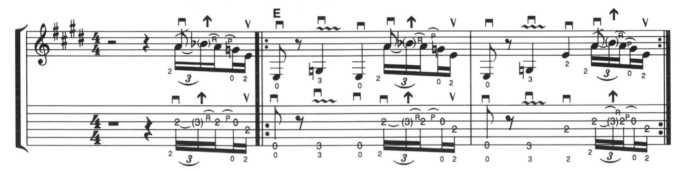

26. Fast Blues Shuffle in A

Here's a great rhythmic sounding riff.

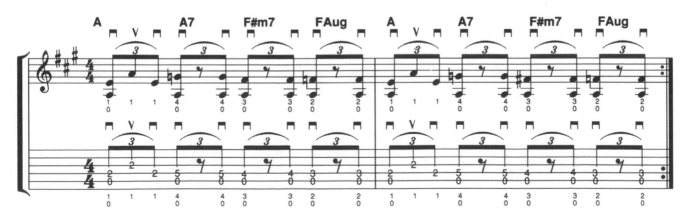

Blues Intros/Outros and Turnarounds
27. Intro In G

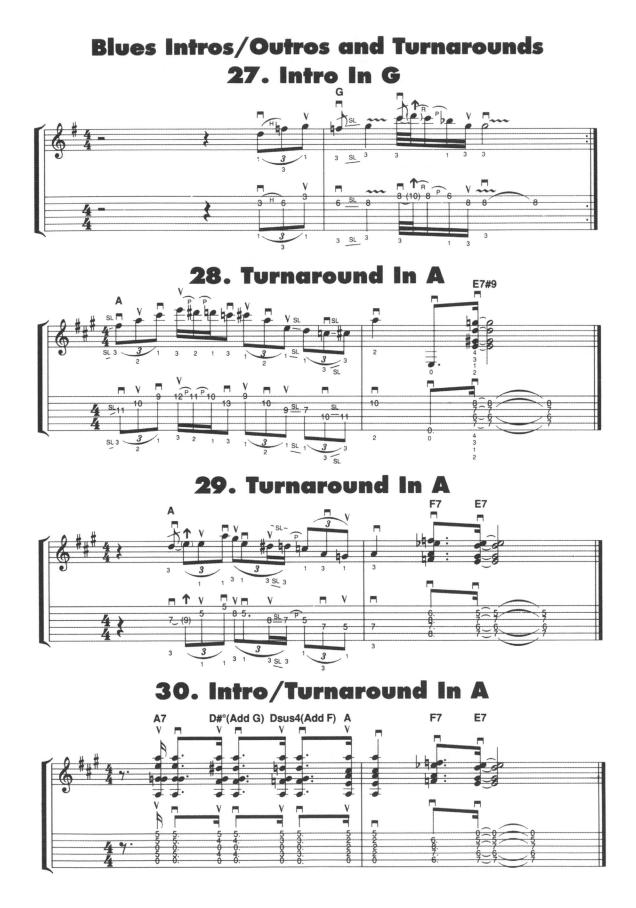

28. Turnaround In A

29. Turnaround In A

30. Intro/Turnaround In A

31. Outro In C

32. Outro In C

33. Intro In G

34. Outro In G

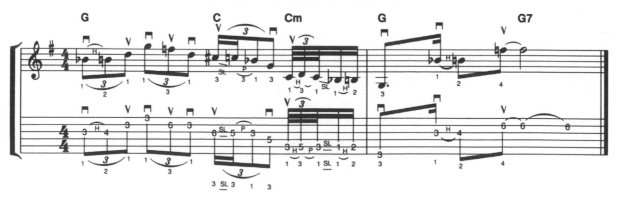

Going Out Blues
written by Alan Warner

Because I wanted to improvise this guitar solo to get a bluesy feel, I recorded it
before writing the music. This means that some parts may differ slightly from the
recorded version. You may of course like to improvise on the material anyway. At the
end of section 1 (measure 13) you will see Lick No. 16 (G Blues Lick), which brings
you into section 2. The next two measures are pretty fast, and make good use of
hammer-ons, pull-offs and slides to create the feeling of speed.
The 5th measure of Section 3 starts with
Lick No. 19 (C Blues Lick).
In the next measure you will see that in the slide from the 7th to the 8th note your left
hand first finger has to change to your second finger midway.
(This is to get into position for the next note.)
The solo finishes with Lick No. 34 (Outro in G).

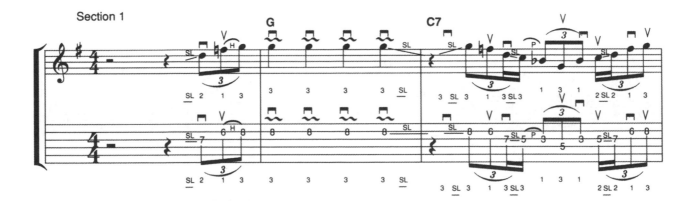

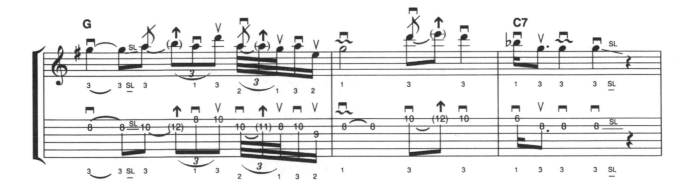

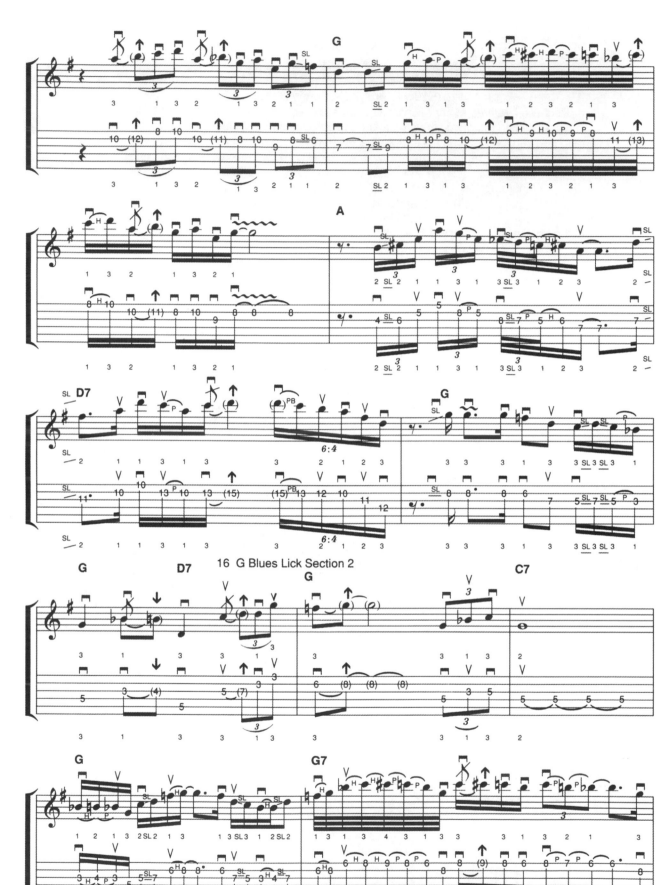

16 G Blues Lick Section 2

Section 3

19 C Blues Lick

34 Outro In G

The G Major Country Scale

G is a very good key for playing country music and the simple "G Country Scale" is
an ideal place to start. There are a few open strings in it,
which give the overall sound a special resonance.

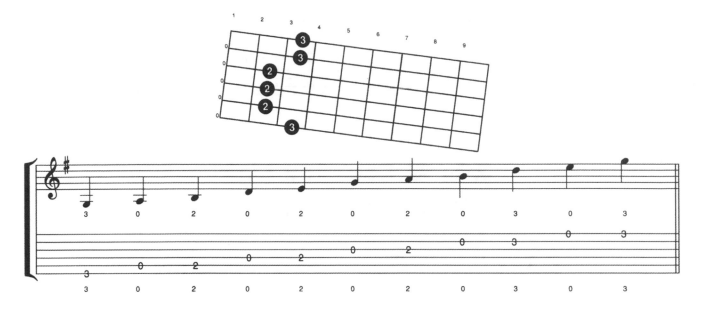

C Major (Double-Note) Country Scale

This double-note country scale can be played with the pick and ring fingers
together or with your thumb and middle fingers together.

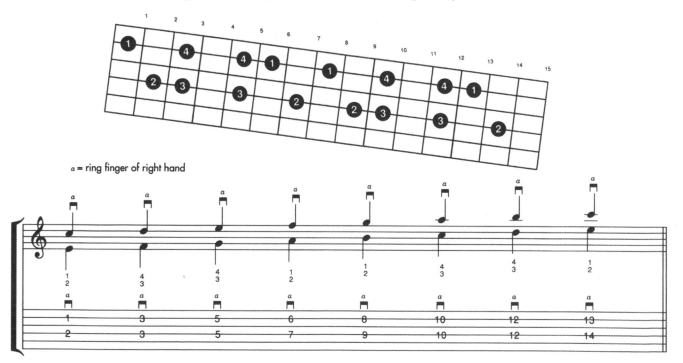

27

35. G Country Lick

This lick is quite easy to play. The notes are from
the G Country Scale.

36. G Country Lick

This lick is also quite easy to play. The notes are from the G Country Scale but with added A# note.
*Pluck the 5th note with your right-hand middle finger (R.H.)`

37. G Country Lick

This lick (combined with the one above),
should be played quite fast.
*(Pluck the 1st, 3rd, 4th and last notes
with right-hand fingers)

*Combining the pick and fingers to sound the notes is a technique used by Albert Lee and Jerry Donahue
amongst others, this is musically very exciting and well worth persevering with to get the right sound.
⊓=Pick, *m*=middle finger and *a*=ring finger.

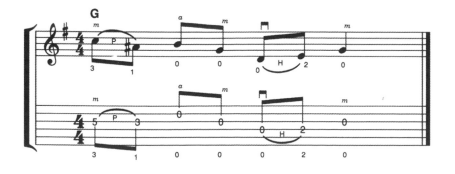

Albert Lee

38. G Country Lick

This lick combines the two previous licks.

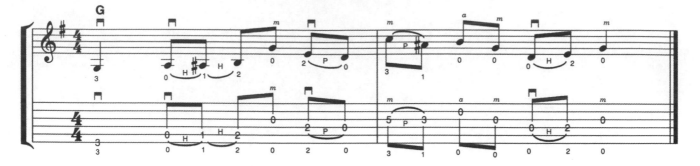

39. Country Lick In C

Use the pick and fingers to strike the strings for this one.

40. Country Lick In C

Play this slowly and exactly in time to give it an old country swing feel.
Use both pick and fingers to sound the notes.

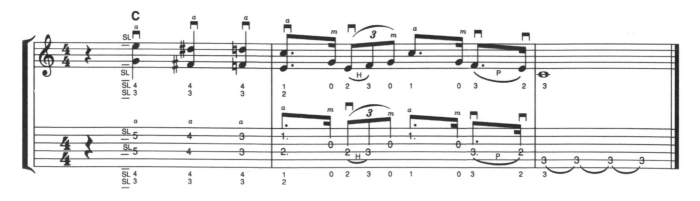

41. Country Lick In C

Here's an interesting lick. In the 3rd measure a chime effect is created by playing the 6th fret of the 2nd string followed by the open 1st string. Use both pick and fingers to sound the notes.

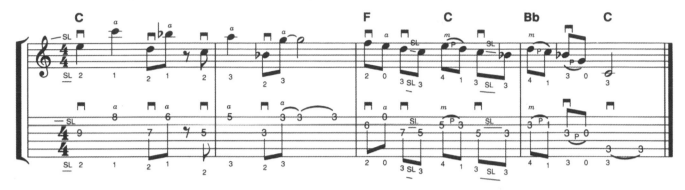

42. Banjo Type Lick In D

You may find this "banjo sound" lick quite difficult as it involves stretching the left hand fingers which form chords. Play with the pick and fingers or thumb and fingers.

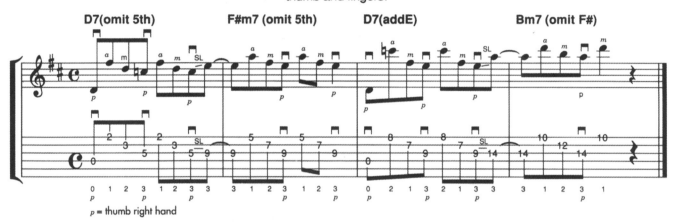

p = thumb right hand

43. Banjo Type Lick In G

This also sounds like a banjo.

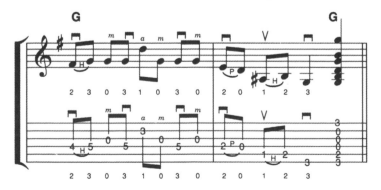

44. Country Rock Lick In A

This lick is similar to The Eagles and The Allman Brothers.

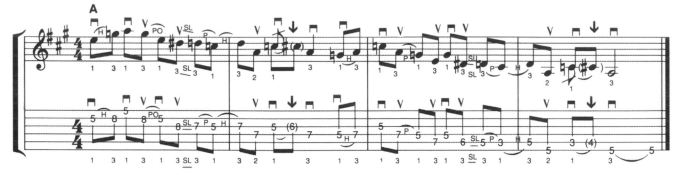

Eagles

45. Country Rock Lick In A

Again this lick is similar to The Eagles and The Allman Brothers.

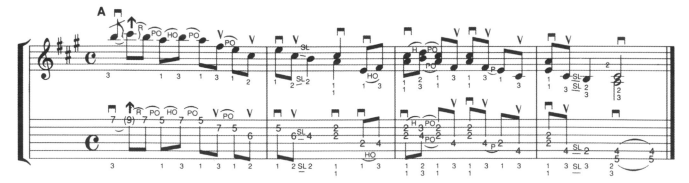

46. Pedal Steel Lick In G

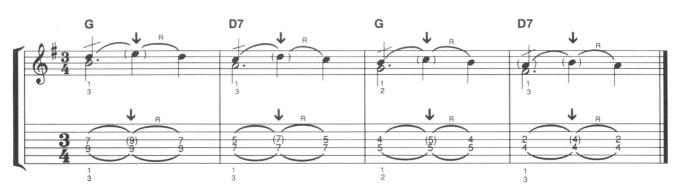

John Denver

47. Pedal Steel Lick In E

Use pick or pick and fingers for this.

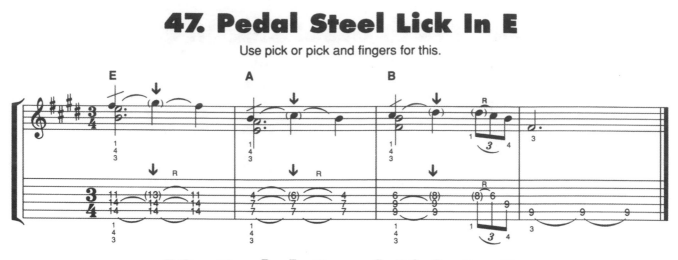

48. Pedal Steel Lick In F

This lick involves the art of playing one bend, holding it, and then playing another on a different string.
First, start an upward string bend on the 7th fret of the 4th string and while still holding it in its upward position, perform a downward string bend on the 5th fret of the third string, then release it and so on.

The Flying Burrito Brothers

Southern Bound
written by Alan Warner

Southern Bound is fairly straightforward, although it should be played quite fast. The tricky bits are as follows:

a) Section 1, 5th measure. Watch the two fret upward string bend using the left-hand middle finger on the 2nd fret of the 3rd string.

b) Section 2. When you start this remember to *combine* picking and playing the strings with your fingers.

c) Section 2, measures 9 and 10. To create a chime effect, play open strings where marked, instead of stopping the notes as you would normally. Combined pick and fingers are required here as well.

d) Section 3. This starts with a two fret string bend, *but* the strings stay bent up for the first two measures. Then release them down to a one fret string bend. (Also combined pick and fingers.)

e) Section 4. This starts with Licks Nos. 36 and 37 (G Country Licks).

f) Section 5. This is the same as Section 1. Outro Lick No. 54 (Outro Lick in G) finishes the solo.

Section 1

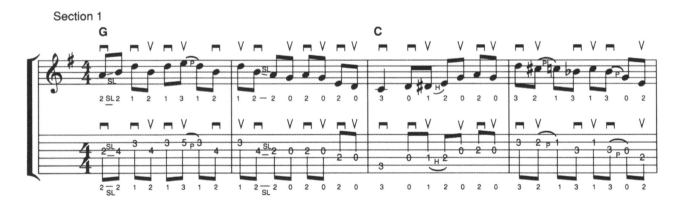

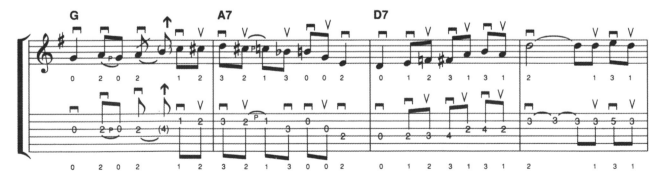

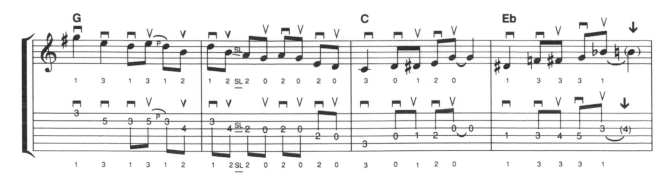

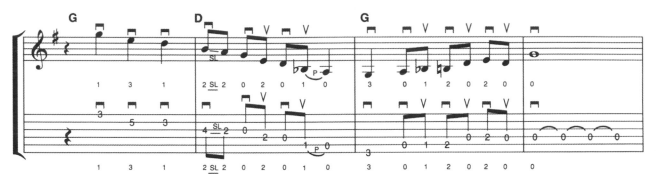

Section 2
43 Banjo Type Lick In G

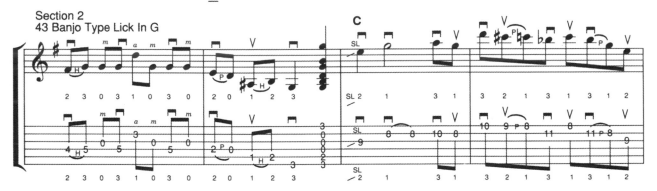

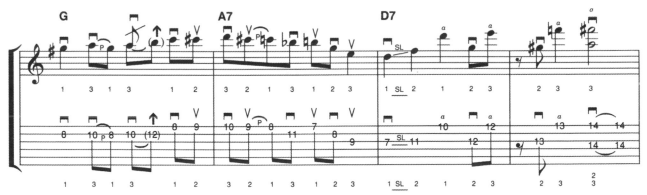

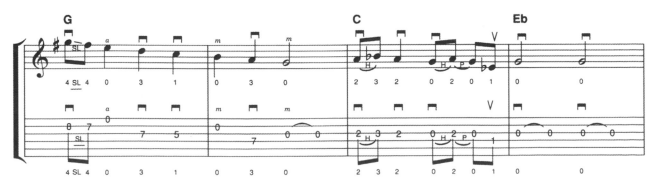

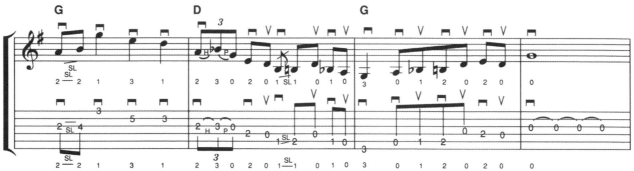

Section 3

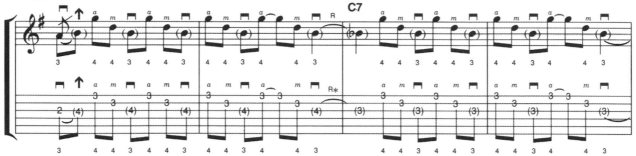

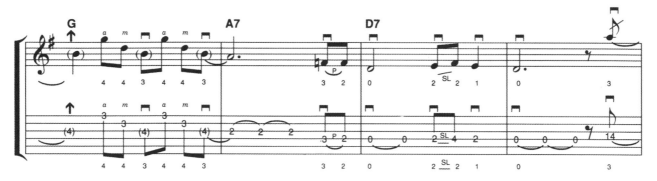

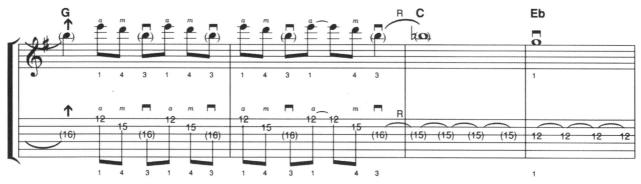

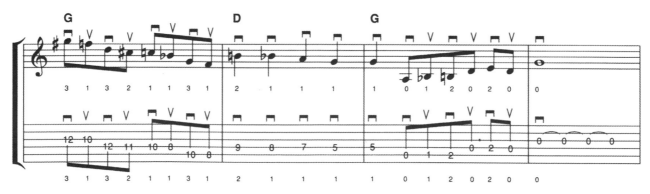

38 G Country Lick
Section 4

Section 5 Same as section 1

38

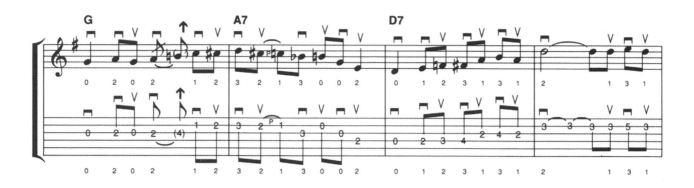

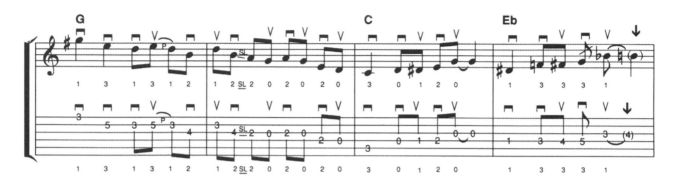

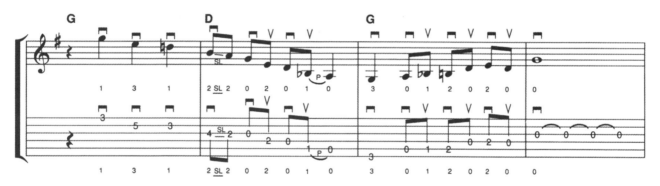

54 Outro in G

To finish

39

Country Intros/Outros and Turnarounds

49. Intro In G

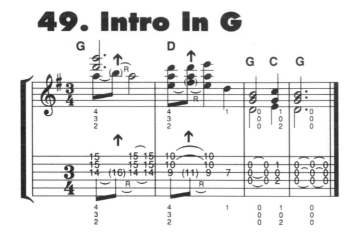

50. Outro In G

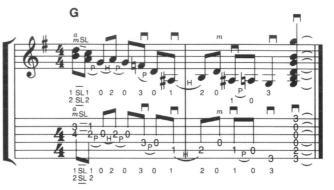

51. Outro In A

52. Outro Lick In C

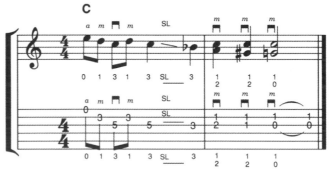

53. Country Rag Turnaround In C

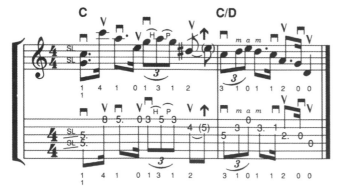

54. Outro In G

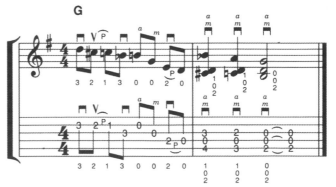

55. Click Note

This percussive effect is extremely useful for funky guitar licks and riffs. It is achieved by striking the strings with the plectrum whilst laying your left-hand fingers lightly across the strings to deaden them.

(For an even more percussive effect try hitting the strings with the palm of your plectrum hand as you strike strings.)

56. Trill

A trill effect is produced by performing hammer-ons and pull-offs in rapid succession. (If you trill one fret apart use your (L.H.) index and ring fingers. If two frets apart use your index and middle fingers.)

57. Click-Note/Trill Exercise

Try the click-notes and the trill in this exercise.
Play it with a staccato feel throughout.

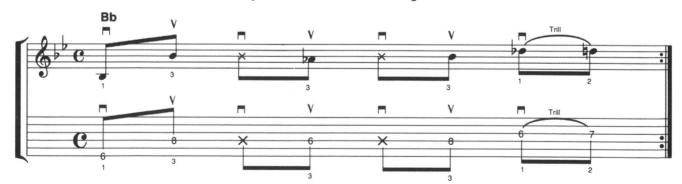

41

58. Funky Riff In Bb

As in No. 57 this lick uses click notes and trills and has a definite staccato feel to it.

59. Bb Funky Riff

Notice the string bend in the last measure.
This has to be played clean and sharp otherwise the effect will be lost.

60. E Funk Riff

Play this riff with a staccato feel.

61. Funky Chord Riff In A

You may find the chord hammer-ons in the first and third measures a bit difficult.
Also the trill in the last measure may need a bit of practice.

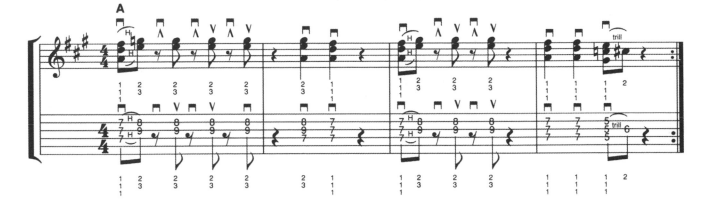

62. Funk Riff In E

The following riff makes effective use of slides.

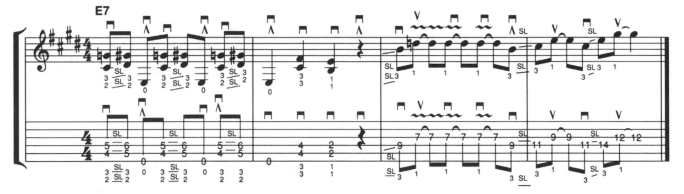

63. Funk Riff In E

Here is a simple but effective riff in E.

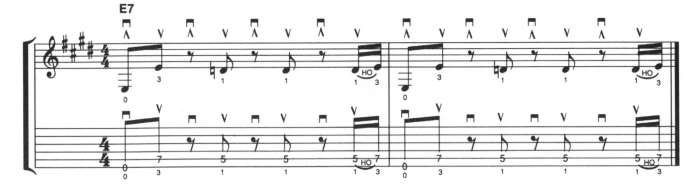

Feelin' Funky
written by Alan Warner

The first Section of this Funk Solo is based on the
'Funk Riff In Bb' No 58.
The middle 8 section relies mainly on chordwork, there are some lead
guitar parts thrown in to 'blend' with the recorded track, these have
been written out separately.

For example, measure
four uses this lead part

Measures eight and nine use this guitar part

Section 1
58 Funky Riff in Bb

Middle 8 section

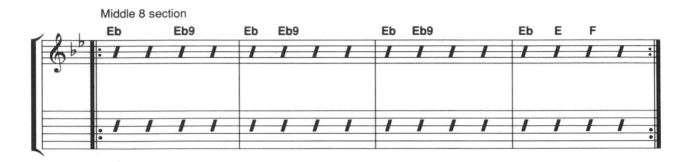

This lead guitar part appears on measures five, six and seven of the first middle 8 section

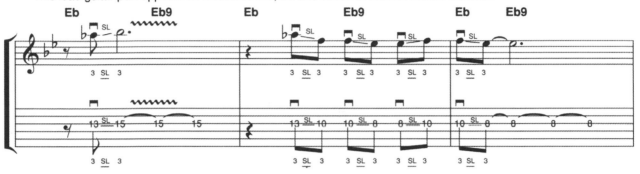

Lead guitar part for measures
four and five (section 1 2nd time round)

Lead guitar part for measure eight
(section 1 2nd time)

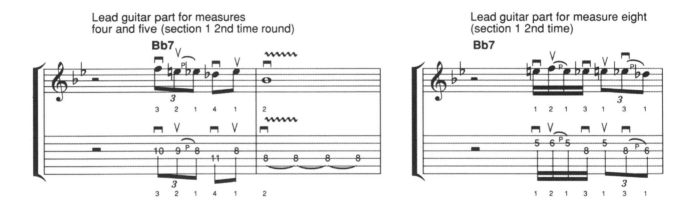

This guitar part is played throughout the 2nd middle 8 section

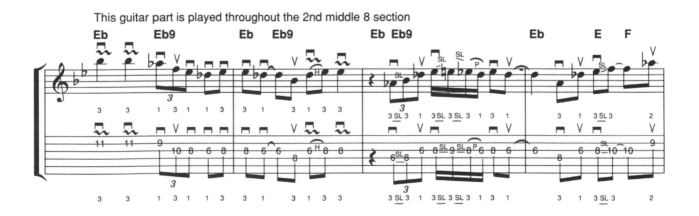

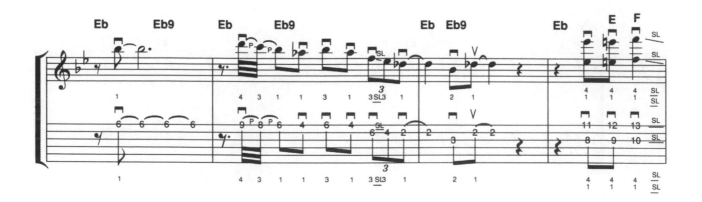

This guitar part is played throughout section 1 3rd time round

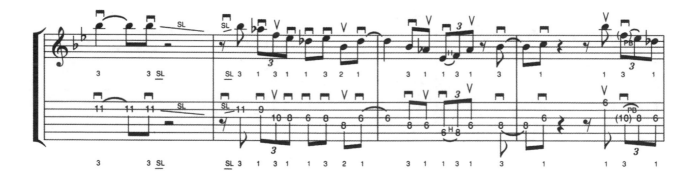

This guitar part is played throughout middle 8 section (3rd time)

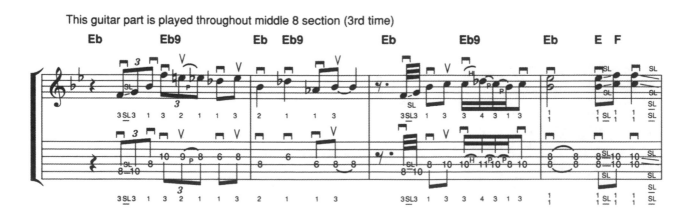

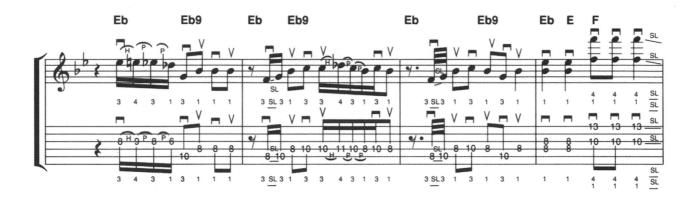

Lead guitar part
on fourth measure
of section 1 (last time)

Lead guitar part
on sixth measure of
section 1 (last time)

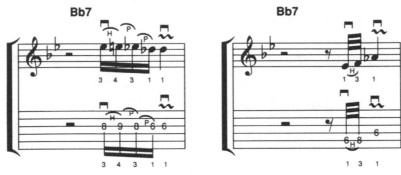

Lead guitar part on measures
eight and nine (Section 1 last time)
Also finishes solo.

Scale Modes

This section concentrates on playing heavy metal guitar, for which these scale modes are essential.
Use them as a regular warm-up routine starting with the G Ionian (G major scale)
and finishing with the Ionian (an octave higher).

64. G Ionian

65. A Dorian

66. B Phrygian

67. C Lydian

68. D Mixolydian

69. E Aeolian

70. F# Locrian

71. G Ionian

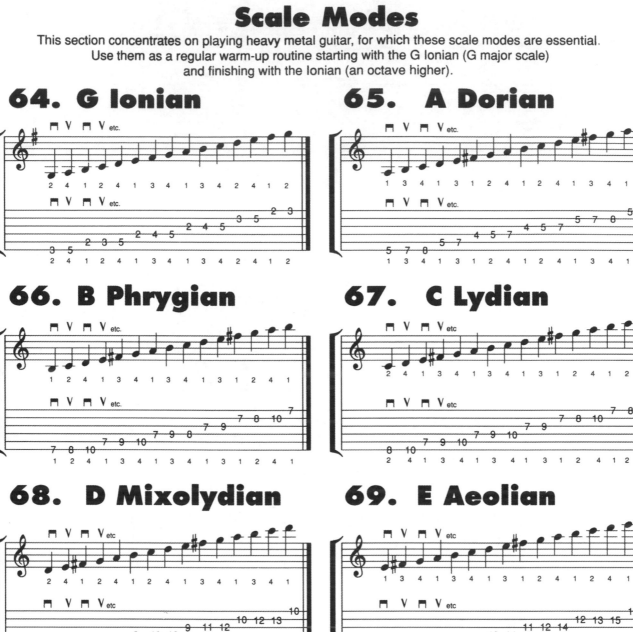

Arpeggios

I've decided to keep these arpeggios in one key to simplify things. Try shifting these positions for other keys.

72. A Major

73. A Minor

74. A Diminished 7th

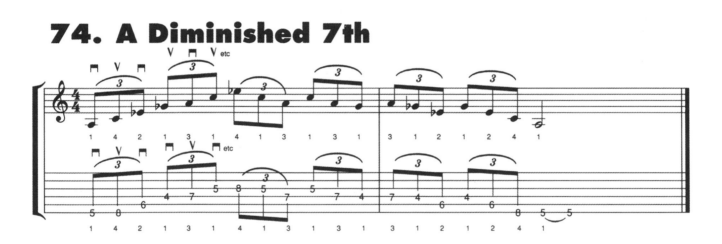

75. A Major Sweep Arpeggio

76. A7

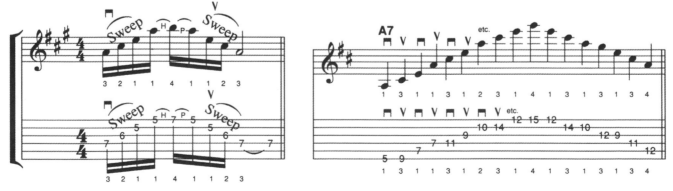

Adrian Smith of Iron Maiden

77. Heavy Metal Lick In A

This exciting Lick starts with an A Power Chord which is followed by some hammer-ons and pull-offs. In the first measure bar the chord with your 1st finger on the 2nd fret and use your 4th finger for the hammer-ons and pull-offs. At the end of the 1st measure slide up to the 9th fret of the third string with your 2nd finger. The rest of the lick is not so difficult.

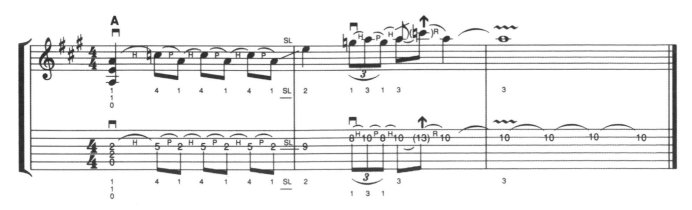

78. Descending Lick In E

The following lick is in the style of Randy Rhoads and Brad Gillis.

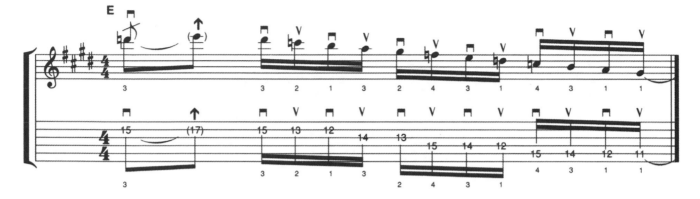

79. Ascending Lick In E7

The next two licks are in the style of Steve Vai and Yngwie Malmsteen. These are great for using towards the end of a guitar solo. The first one is a descending lick and the next is an ascending lick.

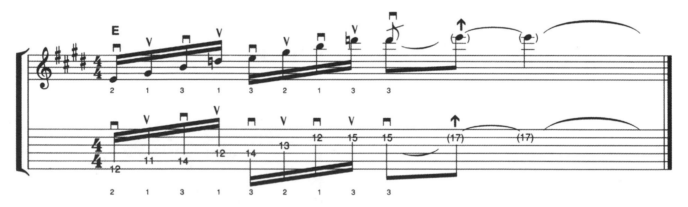

80. Power Chord Riff In A

This is a great riff for providing substance to a song or solo.

81. Power Chord Riff In A

Try counting 1 2 3 1 2 to get the
feel of this 5/4 power chord riff.

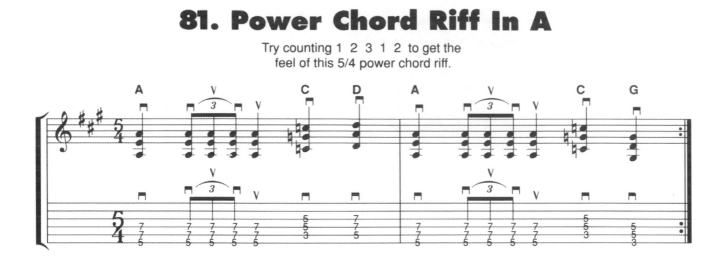

82. Power Chord Riff In D

This power chord riff is similar to the one used on "Down and Out" from the Pluto
album by Pluto. It's quite simple but effective.

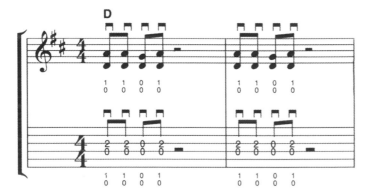

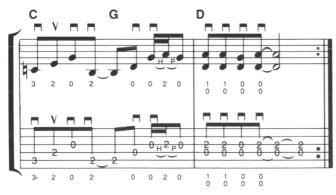

Jimmy Page

Speed Exercises

The following speed exercises have been designed to stretch and strengthen the left-hand fingers as well as improving the right-hand picking technique.

83. Speed Exercise In G

From the G Mixolydian scale/mode

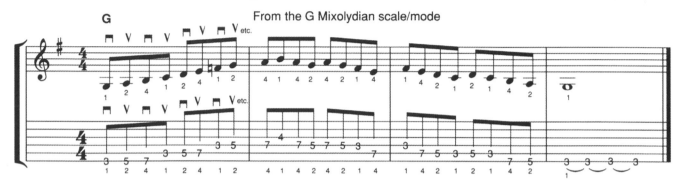

84. Speed Exercise In G

Notes from G harmonic minor scale

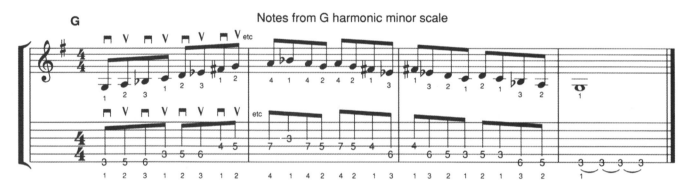

85. Speed Exercise In A

Notes from A major scale

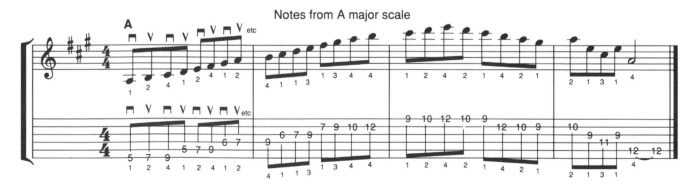

86. Speed Exercise In A minor

Notes from A minor scale

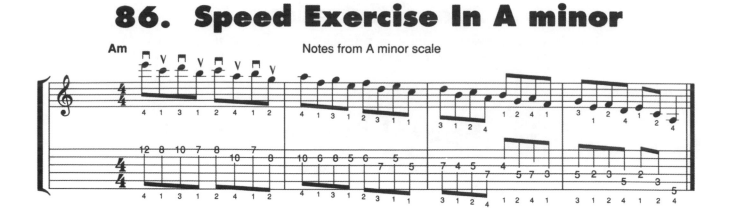

87. Speed Lick In A minor

This very flashy and impressive speed lick
may take a lot of practise.

(Harmonic)

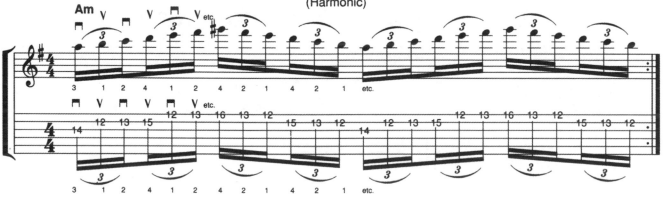

88. Speed Lick In E minor

Here's another flashy lick.
The faster it is played the more effective it sounds.

(Harmonic)

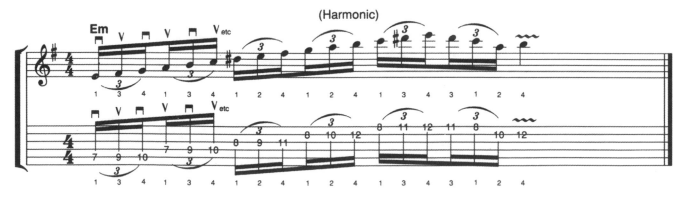

89. Speed Lick In D minor

This lick has you coming down the fingerboard against a Dm to C to Abdim to E resolving on an A Power Chord.

90. Speed Lick In D minor

Notice the classical influence in this lick starting with the 'uncertain' notes over a D minor chord in the first measure, the second measure starts with an arpeggio over an A(b9) chord finally resolving onto a triumphant D major chord.

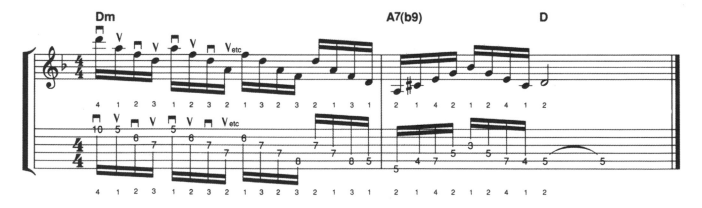

Two-hand Fretting

Right-hand hammer-ons enable you to play notes incredibly fast and smooth in such a way that would be impossible in this conventional playing style, also you can cover a greater span of the frets.

91. Right-hand Hammer-on

In this exercise start by fretting the second note in readiness. Then hammer your right-hand index or middle finger onto the first note, and as you release the note, pick the string RP with the same finger, which will then sound the next note. Next hammer-on in the normal way.

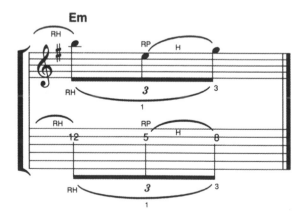

92. Right-hand Hammer-on

This exercise begins with a right-hand pick RP on the first note followed by a 'normal' hammer-on RH then a right-hand hammer-on.

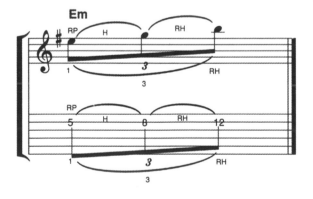

Eddie Van Halen

Two-hand Fretting

93. Right-hand 'Capo'

Place your right-hand index finger on the 4th fret of the 3rd string (this is the capo position) now hammer-on to the 9th fret with the left-hand 3rd finger. Then pull off onto the 7th fret and finally the 4th fret which is the right-hand capo position.

94. Right-hand 'Capo' Slam

'Slam' your right-hand index finger onto the 4th fret of the 3rd string (RH capo slam.) Then hammer-on to the next note with the 1st finger (left-hand). Then hammer on to the last note (left-hand 3rd finger).

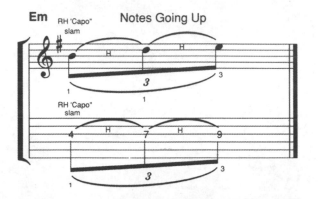

Van Halen

95. Right-hand Hammer-on Lick
In A minor

Now try this right-hand hammer-on lick which is quite easy really. All you have to do in the second measure is to move your left-hand position down one fret.

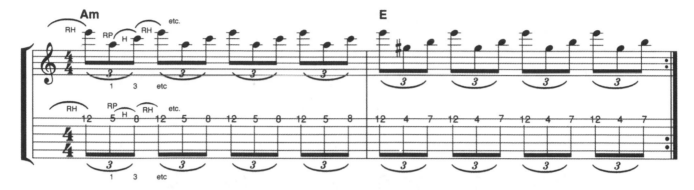

96. Right-hand Hammer-on Lick In E

You will have to stretch your
left-hand fingers (index and 4th) here

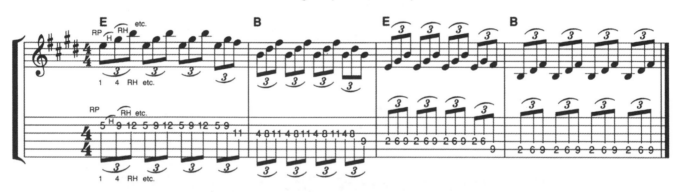

97. Right-hand Hammer-on Lick In G

Start slowly on this one as it's quite impressive once you've mastered it.

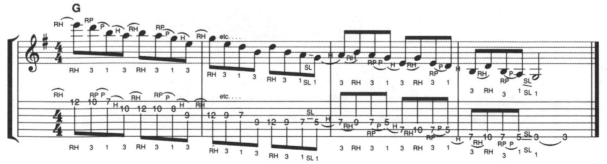

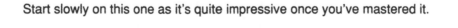

98. Right-hand Hammer-on Lick In A

This lick starts with a 2 fret bend on the 4th fret of the 3rd string and is followed by a right-hand hammer-on (7th fret). It is important at this stage that you keep this string bent up so the 7th fret will sound 2 frets higher. Then release the bend back to the original note. It should be fairly straightforward after this.

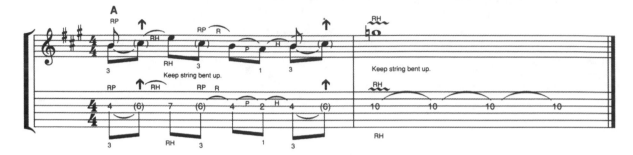

99. Right-hand Capo Slam In A

This lick starts with a right-hand capo slam followed by two hammer-ons and a string bend. While the string is still bent up perform a right-hand hammer-on for the last note.

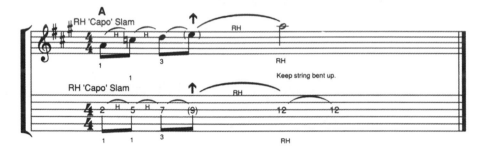

100. Right-hand Capo Lick In D

Now we come to the final lick, which starts with a right-hand 'capo' in readiness for the triplet notes (1st measure). Then a two-fret string bend is followed by a right-hand hammer-on (keep string bent up). Release bend and pull-off twice to go back to capo position. Finally hammer-on to the next note and bend string up to the last note.

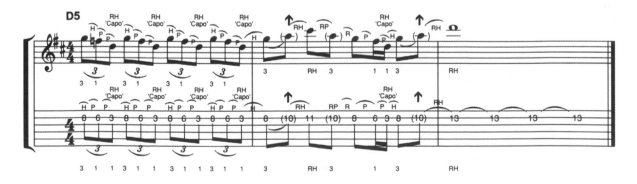

Time For Change
written by Alan Warner

Here's a solo that makes full use of scales, arpeggios, speed licks
and right-hand fretting, as well as slides, string bending, hammer ons,
pull offs, trills and vibratos.
The intro starts with a descending run based on the
A Spanish Flamenco Scale.
(A A# C# D E F G)
There is no fixed tempo here and that's why there are no tails or
beams to join the notes together. A slide from the 5th to the 9th fret of
the 6th string starts an A Major Arpeggio, which is followed by a
diminished 7th run resolving onto a D power chord.
Next comes No. 77 (Heavy Metal Lick in A) to finish the Intro.
The Lead Guitar in sections 1 2 and 3 is played over Lick No. 80
(Power Chord Riff).
The Middle 8 sections are made up of C7, D7 and E7 arpeggios
(in the same format as in Lick No. 76 [A7 Arpeggio]).
Notice Lick No. 87 (A Minor [Harmonic Speed Lick]) in Section 2.
The solo finishes with an A Power Chord.

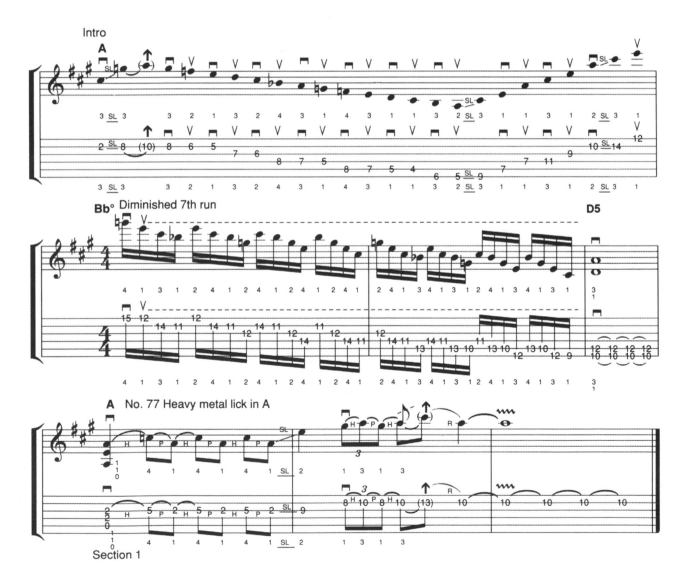

No. 80 Power chord Riff played underneath lead guitar throughout this section.

Middle 8 section

62

Section 2
Power chord riff played underneath lead guitar throughout section.

87 Speed lick in A minor   (Harmonic)

Middle 8 section

Section 3